GRIEF RELIEF

from the Bible:

**A Workbook on
Finding Strength
in Times of Loss**

by John Cunyus

ISBN: 978-1-936497-36-2

Scriptures taken from
THE LATIN TESTAMENT PROJECT BIBLE
(Used by permission)

Liturgical Contribution from
The Rev Michael LaRue, S.T.M.

October 18, 2017
©2017, John G. Cunyus
All Rights to the Images, and Commentary Reserved,
except as noted.
Photos by John Cunyus

Searchlight Press
Who are you looking for?
Publishers of thoughtful Christian books since 1994.
PO Box 554
Henderson, TX 75652-0554
214.662.5494
www.Searchlight-Press.com
www.JohnCunyus.com

Table of Contents

Introduction

There is no magic pill to make grief go away. We must deal with it directly and patiently.

We live in the midst of what some are calling "The Great Falling Away" from Christian faith in the United States. People no longer go to church as a matter of course. Larger and larger portions of the society around seem immune to this age-old Good News. In the midst of all that, I was sitting in my office at the church on a hot Summer day, wondering how to reach others more effectively with the love of Jesus Christ.

Just then, I happened to scroll across a series of suggestions on reaching others for Christ, written by Southeastern Seminary professor Dr. Chuck Lawless, Jr. One of his suggestions was to address the need for grief support in our communities. However fractured our society may be, grief is one experience nearly all of us have in common. Furthermore, secular societies like our own often have trouble helping the grieving. At some point in grief, the distractions cease to distract, the denials ring hollow, and the medications stop working. With that came a realization I've felt many times before: if what we put our faith in does not help us deal with grief, we need to find something that does!

It felt like a lightbulb turned on in my heart. I immediately began going through the Bible, looking up references to grief and grieving. I found 104 passages mentioning grief, from the first book of the Bible to the last. Jeremiah, the "weeping prophet," led all others with 13 references. Genesis, at the beginning, addressed the topic 11 times. Clearly, grieving has been with us a long time, and the Biblical witness takes it seriously.

As I gathered each of these passages, I felt the good Lord addressing something my own heart needed. These passages addressed grief not in an obsolete fashion, but in ways that seem relevant and vital, even today. As I summarized each of the passages and drew insights from them, the Word enlightened my own grief, giving me tools for dealing with it constructively. I pray it does the same for you.

This book is divided into two sections.
1. The first section defines grief, provides opportunities for detailing our own grief, then outlines some biblical and secular approaches for dealing with it.
2. The second section contains the 104 grief passages from the Bible, with brief attached descriptions and questions to help you go deeper.

I hope in presenting these passages on grief that we recognize ourselves in them. Seeing how the Bible describes grief and its causes, we see also the ways it connects to our experience. We take the necessary comforts from it. Dragging the causes of our grief out of the shadows and into the light is often a huge step in moving forward from it.

Above all, I hope that the process of dealing with our own grief reconnects us to Jesus Christ and to the community gathered around Him. He, through His life, death, and Resurrection, is the One who transforms our grief into glory.

John Cunyus

What Is Grief?

From www.Dictionary.com: Grief is "keen mental suffering or distress over affliction or loss; sharp sorrow; painful regret."

From www.Wikipedia.com: "Grief is a multifaceted response to loss, particularly to the loss of someone or something that has died, to which a bond or affection was formed. Although conventionally focused on the emotional response to loss, it also has physical, cognitive, behavioral, social, cultural, and philosophical dimensions. While the terms are often used interchangeably, bereavement refers to the state of loss, and grief is the reaction to that loss. Grief is a natural response to loss."

From www.MedicineNet.com: "The normal process of reacting to a loss. The loss may be physical (such as a death), social (such as divorce), or occupational (such as a job). Emotional reactions of grief can include anger, guilt, anxiety, sadness, and despair. Physical reactions of grief can include sleeping problems, changes in appetite, physical problems, or illness."

From www.merriam-webster.com: "...deep and poignant distress caused by or as if by bereavement (his grief over his son's death)...a cause of such suffering (life's joys and griefs)

From www.Grief.com: "What is Grief? Grief is the internal part of loss, how we feel. The internal work of grief is a process, a journey. It does not end on a certain day or date. It is as individual as each of us. Grief is real because loss is real. Each grief has its own imprint, as distinctive and as unique as the person we lost. The pain of loss is so intense, so heartbreaking, because in loving we deeply connect with another human being, and grief is the reflection of the connection that has been lost."

Brief Grief Questionnaire

1. **Are You Grieving?**

2. **What Are You Grieving?**

3. **When did your Grief begin?**

Ten Types of Grief in Scripture

Type of Grief	Sufferer	On Behalf of...
Grief for sin	The Lord	Humanity
Grief for a spouse	Abraham	Sarah
Grief for a parent	Isaac	Sarah
Grief for a child	Jacob	Joseph
Anticipatory **Grief**	Jacob	Benjamin
Grief for a friend	David	Jonathan
Grief for a leader	Egypt and Israel	Joseph
Misdirected **Grief**	Jonah	Ivy, not Nineveh
Grief for neighbors	Isaiah	lazer
Grief for possessions	Moab	Material things

Grief Relief from the Bible, 5

Seven Take-Aways for Grief Relief

1. **Grief is a godly emotion.** God felt it first. When you grieve, you aren't alone.
       Original Example: God, for humanity.

2. **Make a memorial** for the one you grieve.
       Original Example: Abraham, for Sarah.

3. **Grief is eased** by love.
       Original Example: Isaac, for Sarah and with Rebecca.

4. **Grief for a child** can be life-long.
       Original Example: Jacob, for Joseph.

5. **Grief recovery** cannot be rushed.
       Original Example: Jacob, with his surviving children.

6. **Grief often diminishes** with time and activity.
       Original Example: Judah, losing his wife, the daughter of Suah.

7. **Anticipating grief changes us,** yet we can choose whether it changes us for the better or not.
       Original Examples: Jacob, for Benjamin; and Judah, for Jacob.

Grief Relief from the Bible, 6

Secular Approaches

Five Stages of Grief
by Elisabeth Kübler-Ross
originally from
<u>On Death and Dying</u>
(Scribner, 1969)

1. Denial
2. Anger
3. Bargaining
4. Depression
5. Acceptance

from
www.Grief.com

"Because Love Never Dies"

The 7 Stages of Grief
Recover-from-Grief.com

1. Shock & Denial
2. Pain & Guilt
3. Anger & Bargaining
4. Depression, Reflection, Loneliness
5. The Upward Turn
6. Reconstruction & Working Through
7. Acceptance & Hope

from
www.recover-from-grief.com
http://www.recover-from-grief.com/7-stages-of-grief.html

Steps in Overcoming Anxiety
Since grief and anxiety often go hand in hand,
these suggestions may also come in handy.

1. Name the feeling.
"This is anxiety that I'm feeling.
This is grief that I'm feeling."

2. Look for the sources.
"I'm grieving because of ..."

3. See your situation as it really is.
"I'm alive. I have these resources.
I am not defenseless."

4. Be kind to yourself.
"Don't say or do anything to yourself
that you wouldn't say or do politely
to someone else in the same situation."

5. Remember that anxious thoughts and memories are just thoughts and memories.
"That scary thought I just had is just a thought.
That painful memory is just a memory.
These things don't define me."

6. Replace negative 'what ifs' with positive ones.
"Good things are as likely to happen as bad.
Imagine the good happening, not just the bad."

7. Do something constructive; don't just sit there.
"Even if it's something small, do it!"

Grief Insights from Genesis

Grief is the necessary shadow of love.
If we didn't love, we wouldn't grieve.

God created humanity in love, taking upon Himself the possibility of grief. Genuine love cannot be compelled. It can merely be evoked. By creating in us the freedom to love, God creates at the same time the freedom <u>not</u> to love, the freedom to turn away.

God is the first One to grieve on earth. He grieves over sin:

- which leads those He loves to destruction;
- which causes us to abuse the freedom He created, thereby intensifying the pain of the world.

Who grieves?

The Lord grieves.

Human beings grieve.

Peoples and nations grieve.

What causes their grief?

Human wickedness is the first cause of grief in Genesis.

Loss also causes grief:
> of a spouse
> of a parent
> of a child
> of a revered family member, friend, leader

What helps with grief?

Appropriate memorializing and mourning of the dead (as with Abraham)

New love (as with Isaac)

Returning after an appropriate time to prior routines (as with Judah)

Restoration of the one lost (as with Joseph)

What does not help with grief?

Trying to rush someone through it (as with Jacob)

Manipulating someone else's grief for our own purposes (as with Esau)

What is Anticipatory Grief?

Grief isn't always over something that has already happened. Some grief is anticipatory (as with Jacob and Benjamin). Because of what we have already experienced, we anticipate greater grief in the future if something similar should occur.

Is anticipatory grief always a bad thing?

Not necessarily. Sometimes anticipating another's grief brings out the best in us (as with Judah and with Pharaoh.) In fact, anticipatory grief may be a great blessing to us, if we take it to heart.

Four Lessons Grief Teaches Us

1. Grief teaches us the value of love.
Sometimes we don't know how much we love someone until we lose them. On the other hand, sometimes we don't know how harmful someone else is to us until they are gone as well.

2. Grief teaches us what our priorities are.
Somehow, things like answering the latest email, seeing a hot movie, buying that new iPhone, or wearing those killer shoes don't matter as much as we thought they did, once our grief begins.

3. Grief teaches us how precious memories are.
We realize how much the time and memories we made together mattered. Sometimes we also realize how little time we actually took to make memories.

4. Grief teaches us to turn to the Lord.
Ultimately, only the Lord can console our grief.

ALL of these are lessons we could take to heart before we have to grieve.
Will we?

Two Ways of Prayer
Many people find that being able pray is a great help in times of grief.
Here are two simple patterns for doing so.

A PATTERN FOR PRAYER

Reflect on a passage from scripture. Let its meaning lead you into God's presence.
Praise God's greatness.
Ask God's forgiveness for your sins and offer your forgiveness to others for theirs. God has promised to forgive you as you forgive others.
Lift Up the needs of others. Be specific, and name names. Pray for the sick and the lost, for your family, church, and friends, and for the world.
Share your own concerns, holding nothing back. Clear your mind and heart. Ask for what you need. Be honest.
Give Thanks, whatever the situation may be. In Christ there is always a blessing.

A WAY OF MEDITATIVE PRAYER

1. Sit comfortably. Breathe slowly and evenly, paying attention to each breath as it comes and goes. (See Genesis 2:7)

2. With each breath, repeat the phrase: *The Lord is my shepherd.* When you find your mind wandering, gently bring your focus back to the breathing and prayer.

3. Set a timer and do this for five to ten minutes during the day, to center your soul on the God of scripture.

An Order of Public Prayer for the Grieving
by the Rev Michael LaRue, S.T.M.

To be said by oneself, or with others. If by oneself, then the leader's part is prayed like the others, without change.

At the beginning, if you are mourning over a person, keep some quiet time, and ask God to show you how you may have sinned against that person. Then ask God to forgive you. Then consider before God how the other person may have hurt you, whether intentionally or not, and then tell God that you forgive that person for these hurts.

All begin   Almighty God, I confess that I have sinned against you, in thought, word, and deed, by what I have done, and by what I have left undone, through my fault, my own fault, my own most grievous fault. Trusting in your mercy given in your Son, our Lord Jesus Christ, I ask you to have mercy upon me, forgive me my sins, and give me the grace to amend my life so that it may be pleasing to you. This I pray through Jesus Christ our Lord. Amen.

Leader   Almighty God, who has promised forgiveness of sins to all who with hearty repentance and true faith turn to him, have mercy upon us, pardon all our sins, and bring us to eternal life, through Jesus Christ our Lord.

All   Amen.

Leader   O God, make speed to save me.

Response   O Lord, make haste to help me.

All *Glory to the Father, and to the Son,*
and to the Holy Spirit:
As it was in the beginning,
is now and will be for ever. Amen.

Blessed are those who mourn:
for they will be consoled.

Vulgate Psalm 38

1 I said, "I will guard my ways, that I not fall short through my tongue."
I placed my mouth under guard when *a* sinner stood up against me.

2 I became silent and was humbled. I grew quiet, apart from good, and my pain was renewed.

3 My heart grew hot inside me, and fire will blaze forth in my meditation. I said in my tongue,

4 "Make my end known to me, Lord, and who is *the* number of my days, so I may know what is lacking to me!"

5 Look! You established my days' measures. My substance *is* like nothing before You. All *the* same, every living man is all vanity.

6 Even so, man passes through in appearance, yet is troubled even for no reason. He gathers treasures, yet does not know for whom he will gather them.

7 Now, what is my expectation? Isn't it *the* Lord? My substance is with You.

8 Rescue me from all my iniquities! You have given me *a* fool's shame.

9 I kept silent and didn't open my mouth because You did.

10 Take Your beatings away from me! I have been destroyed in rebukes from Your hand's strength.

11 Because of iniquity, You have corrected man, and made his soul dry up like *a* spider's web. Nevertheless, each man is troubled vainly.

12 Hear my prayer, Lord! Understand my petition with ears! Do not silence my tears, because I am *a* stranger with You, *a* pilgrim, like all my fathers!

13 Send me back that I may be refreshed, before I go away and will be no more!

Glory to the Father, and to the Son,
and to the Holy Spirit:
As it was in the beginning,
is now and will be for ever. Amen.

> Blessed are those who mourn:
> for they will be consoled.

Leader A reading from Isaiah *(Isaiah 61:1-3)* The Lord's breath is on me, because the Lord has anointed me to preach to the gentle. He sent me to heal the shattered in heart, that I might proclaim pardon to the captive, and opening to the closed in; that I might proclaim the year of the Lord's appeasing, and the day of vengeance to our God; that I might console all the grieving; that I might appoint Sion to the grieving, and give them a crown for ashes, joy's oil for weeping, praise's covering for a mourning breath. They will be called mighty ones of righteousness in it, the Lord's planting, to glorifying.

> But you, O Lord, have mercy on us.

All Thanks be to God

Leader Lord, you have paid the debt for all our sins. We gratefully offer our suffering and grief to you, for our sins and those of others, especially those for whom we mourn, asking you to transform us and use our pain to our healing and your glory.

All Lord, have mercy.

Leader Lord, we know that you love us all, wish us to be healed from sin and all its effects, and to reign with you in your Kingdom. We know that you are all powerful. Therefore we entrust ourselves and those we love (especially _________) to your never-ending care and love, knowing that you can and will do what is best for all to lead them into your Kingdom.

All Lord, have mercy.

Leader Defend us with your heavenly protection and by the help of your Holy Angels from all the attacks of the Enemy, from despair, loss of trust in you, hatred, desire for revenge, and all destructive thoughts.

All Lord, have mercy.

Leader Lord, we pray for all those who grieve, that we may know your love and comfort.

All Lord, have mercy.

Leader Deliver us, Lord, from all bitterness toward those who have caused us injury, and heal any hurts that we have suffered.

All Lord, have mercy.

Leader Lord, forgive us any ways that we have injured others, help us to make what amends we can, and heal any broken relations.

All Lord, have mercy.

Leader Deliver us from all attachments to the things of this world, and grant that all our loves may be grounded in, and in accordance with, our love for you.

All Lord, have mercy.

Leader We thank you, Lord, for all the blessings you have bestowed upon us, especially through those who have been parted from us *(here take a few minutes silence)* and grant that we may always be thankful and praise you.

All Lord, have mercy.

Leader Now in the words our Savior taught us, let us pray

All

> *Our Father, Who art in heaven,*
> *Hallowed be Thy Name;*
> *Thy kingdom come,*
> *Thy will be done,*
> *on earth as it is in heaven.*
> *Give us this day our daily bread,*
> *and forgive us our trespasses,*
> *as we forgive those who trespass against us;*
> *and lead us not into temptation,*
> *but deliver us from evil.*
> *For thine is the Kingdom, and the power,*
> *and the glory, for ever and ever. Amen.*

Leader. O Lord, hear my prayer.

All　　　　　And let my cry come to you.
Leader　　　　Let us pray.
O merciful Father, who has taught us in your holy Word that you do not willingly afflict or grieve the children of men: Look with pity upon the sorrows of your servants. Remember us, O Lord, in mercy, nourish our souls with patience, comfort us with a sense of your goodness, lift up your countenance upon us, and give us peace; through Jesus Christ our Lord, who lives and reigns with you and the Holy Spirit, God, now and always, and to the ages of ages.
All　　　　　Amen.

Leader　　　　Now to him who by the power at work within us is able to do far more abundantly than all that we ask or think, to him be glory in the church and in Christ Jesus to all generations, for ever and ever.

(Ephesians 3:20)

All　　　　　Amen.

Grief Relief from the Bible, 12

Grief in the Bible

<table><tr><td>

GRIEF IS A GODLY EMOTION!
Consider that, if you are grieving.

</td><td>

The word "Grief" in its various forms appears 63 times in the Revised Standard Version of the Bible.

"Grief" appears in 104 passages in 33 different books in <u>The Latin Testament Project Bible</u>, excluding the Apocrypha.

</td></tr></table>

What follows is a book-by-book survey of the 104 passages dealing with grief, with a one-sentence synopsis at the top of each. As you read through them and consider their contexts, reflect how the grief in the text touches your own.

Grief Relief from the Bible, 13

Grief in Genesis

1. The first grief of all was the Lord's, at humanity's wickedness to one another.

> **Genesis 6:5-6:** "God, seeing that man's great harmfulness was in *the* land and all *the* heart's thought was directed to harm all *the* time, **6:6** it made Him sorry that He had made man in *the* land, and touched *His* heart inside with grief.

I. It is worth our while to pay attention today to the problem of grief. We live in a grievous world. Suffering touches every human life. If what we have faith in does not help us face grief, it's not much use...is it? Let's take a look at grief from a Biblical perspective, because so many are going through so much right now.

II. The first to grieve in scripture was the Lord. This is not what we would expect, given the history of what went before. Perhaps Adam or Eve would have grieved Abel's death and Cain's exile. Yet no word of it appeared in the text.

III. Consider what this tells us about the Lord. Our Lord is capable of grief. He grieved first, not His creation. In fact, grief is the necessary shadow of love, even for God. The only way to avoid grief entirely is to avoid love entirely. That's not worth the trade-off, even for the Lord.

IV. What grieves God? Human harmfulness grieves Him. What does this mean? It is our harmfulness to one another, the terrible suffering human beings inflict on other human beings and on themselves, whether intentionally or not. Does it grieve you?

V. Consider the implications of that. Because this magnificent God loves us and our free love can't be compelled, He respects the freedom of His created children to disappoint Him, to do wrong, to live heedlessly. They were His image, the outpouring of His love. Yet they exercised their freedom to harm one another.

VI. He grieves over what they've become. Do you suppose He still does?

VII. In this case, God grieves the loss of those He created in love. God, who created a moral universe, knows the consequences that follow wickedness. Those consequences come like an overpowering flood. He grieves those whom He created for Himself, who turn away to destruction.

VIII. He grieves possibilities that have been ruined. God is not merely capable of grief; God is the first to grieve.

IX. Yet He does not stop being God! In this passage, He takes the hand of a few, carries them through a catastrophic flood, and reestablishes them on the other side.

X. He does not give up! Wickedness does not end the story. Yet it grieves Him all the same.

XI. Grief is legitimate. God felt it first. In what sense can our grief be godly?

XII. God Himself was the first to grieve. If you are grieving right now, I want you to know God has felt what you are feeling today. You are not alone when you grieve.

Amen.

2. The second grief was Abraham's, for his wife, Sarah.

> **Genesis 23:2:** "[Sarah] died in *the* city of Arbee, which is Hebron, in Canaan's land. Abraham came so he could grieve and weep for her."

I. The first human to grieve in the Bible is Abraham. The story takes place long after the Godly grief expressed in Genesis 6:5-6, long after Adam and Eve, after the flood, and after Noah, his wife, and family.

II. Abraham grieves over his spouse, Sarah.

III. Abraham is also the first person called specifically into a relationship with God. God's people are not exempt from grief. As children of Abraham's calling, they are able to name it, to call it what it is.

IV. Abraham also gives us a model for grieving. He buys a burial plot. He makes a memorial for Sarah. He grieves publicly. Then he carries on with his life. How has this happened in our lives, or in the lives of those we know?

3. The third grief was Isaac's, for his mother, Sarah.

> **Genesis 24:67** *Isaac* brought *[Rebecca]* into Sarah his mother's tent and took her *as* wife. He loved her so much that *the* grief which followed his mother's death was eased.

I. The first person consoled over grief was Isaac.

II. He grieved the loss of his mother, Sarah. If Abraham's grief over the loss of his spouse was the first human grief, the second human grief is that of losing a parent.

III. Isaac's grief is eased through his love for Rebecca, his newlywed wife. The word "eased" is not accidental. It was not erased or forgotten. It did not go away entirely. It was "eased."

IV. Sometimes our expectations about grief get us in trouble.

V. How can we let love ease our grief.

Grief Relief from the Bible, 15

4. The abuse of grief begins with Esau, against Jacob.

> **Genesis 27:41:** Therefore Esau always hated Jacob for *the* blessing with which *the* father blessed him. He said in his heart, "Days of grieving will come for my father, so I can kill Jacob my brother."

I. The first person to misuse grief in scripture was Esau, after being cheated of his father's blessing by his brother Jacob.

II. Jacob has by this point fled from Esau's fury into exile in Syria. Esau knows that the period of grief following his father's death will bring Jacob back to the family. At that point, he plans to kill him.

III. I've always felt a little sorry for Esau. Sometimes the hurts we inflict on others in childhood and youth can hurt for a long, long time.

IV. Esau is not the only one who carries old wounds from youth.

V. Certain things that happened to us in our youth, that disadvantaged us, that hurt us, we will never entirely put behind us. For Esau and Jacob, at least, those things became less important as the years went by. They grew up, they saw more of life, they remembered more than just the harm done.

VI. Jacob escaped into long years of exile, far from home and family. Esau stumbled into painful marriages, alienation from his family, and an exile of his own.

VII. Yet when Jacob and Esau reunited after twenty years, they appeared to do so as brothers, not as enemies. That gives me hope.

VIII. It is possible to abuse grief...to use it to do harm...to use it as an excuse...to use it to take advantage. Grief is a godly emotion. Yet we have that terrible freedom which manifests itself so often in life: the freedom to misuse God's gift Do we? Do others that we know? How do we guard against it?

5. The next human grief was Jacob's, for his son, Joseph.

> **Genesis 37:33-34:** When *his* father looked at it, he said, "This is my son's tunic. *A* wild animal has eaten him. *A* beast has devoured Joseph." **37:34** Tearing his clothes, he dressed in sackcloth, grieving his son *a* long time.

I. The next person to grieve in scripture is the above-mentioned Jacob, having been deceived by his other children into believing his son Joseph had been killed by a wild animal. In fact, the other children had kidnaped Joseph and sold him into slavery in Egypt.

II. The third human grief is over the loss of a child.

III. Do we or does someone we know grieve over a child? How does this impact life?

6. Grieving for a child cannot be entirely extinguished, despite attempts to do so.

> **Genesis 37:35** Even though all his children *were* gathering so they could ease *their* father's pain, he did not want to take comfort. He said, "I will go down to *the* inferno grieving my son."

I. The first person to refuse to be prematurely comforted from grief is also Jacob.
II. The grieving are unable to rush through grief, despite the impatience of others.

Blessed *are those* who mourn,
for they will be consoled.
Matthew 5:5

I. Let's look together at the first three human griefs in scripture, and then at what the Bible counsels for dealing with them. The examples are these: Abraham, who lost his wife, Sarah; Isaac, who lost his mother; and Jacob, who lost his son, Joseph. They represent the three primal human griefs: loss of a spouse, loss of a parent, and loss of a child.

II. Abraham lost his wife, Sarah, after at least 62 years of marriage. They had moved together from Ur, near the Persian gulf, to Haran, to Canaan, to Egypt, then back to Canaan. They had endured together years of childlessness. I imagine there were times when Sarah thought Abraham was crazy. Then God answered their fervent prayer and gave them a son together, Isaac, born in their old age. Then, Sarah had nearly lost Isaac when God tested her husband. At long last, after all that, Sarah died, and Abraham was left alone. It is the first time in scripture a human being explicitly grieves. How do you deal with losing someone who has been your partner, your soul mate, bone of your bones and flesh of your flesh for over sixty years? Abraham may have been the first to grieve such a circumstance, but he certainly wasn't the last.

III. The second human grief is Isaac's, for his mother. Isaac was loved as only an only child of elderly parents can be. That bond was intensified when God tested Abraham's faith, after Abraham had wavered. Then, as will happen to most, the parent died, and the child was left to grieve.

IV. The third human grief is Jacob's, for his son Joseph. Jacob had sent his 16 year-old, second-youngest son and favorite on his first solo outing, to check on his brothers. A while later, ten of Jacob's other sons come to him, carrying Joseph's torn, bloody tunic. Jacob grieves wildly for his son. Even when his other children gather around him, he refuses to be consoled, saying, "*I will go down to the inferno grieving my son.*" I don't believe there is any grief like that of a parent for a child.

V. Yet even as scripture reveals these griefs, it reveals ways to cope with them. Abraham grieves Sarah by coming to her side, buying, then building a memorial to her. In fact, that memorial remains to this day. It highlights, though, the first human response to grief, which is to make a memorial for the one lost. Whether large or small, elaborate or plain, the memorial is a place where we can feel connected to the one we lost. That still matters.

VI. Isaac, grieving his mother, shows us a second response. After Sarah's death, Isaac marries Rebecca. The text tells us, "*He loved her so much that the grief which followed his mother's death was eased.*" New love does not erase old love. It <u>"eases"</u> the loss, however. I believe that's important. Many times grief does not end. I've known folks who still grieve losses from 50, 60 years ago. Yet new love "eases" it. It may be too much to ask for our grief to disappear. But time and love will ease it, if we allow it to.

VII. The third example, Jacob grieving his son Joseph, is both the most terrible and the most hopeful. Jacob does not know that Joseph isn't really dead. He does not know what was even more terrible: that the same sons trying to comfort him are the ones who betrayed and sold their own brother into slavery, then lied to their father for 20 years to cover it up. Jacob refuses consolation, and indeed, that pain is one that never truly goes away.

VIII.. Yet Joseph is not really dead. In fact, after his brothers' terrible crime against him, Joseph rises from the slavery he was sold into up to the highest power in Egypt, where God places him so he may save the very brothers who betrayed him. Is this literal, or symbolic? Yes! Both.

IX. Those loved ones we lose in faith are only gone from our sight, not annihilated. They are in God's hands. By the promise of Jesus Himself, the time will come when they are restored to us, and we to them. The deepest answer to grief for the Christian is that "*death is swallowed up in victory.*" May it be so for us.
Amen.

7. Life goes on, despite our grief.

> **Genesis 37:35b-36:** While [Jacob] continued to cry, **37:36** *the* Midianites sold Joseph in Egypt to Potiphar, Pharaoh's eunuch, *a* military instructor.

I. The first indication that the world goes on despite our grief happens in the story of Joseph being sold as a slave as his father mourns over him in Canaan.

II. This can be a painful realization when we are the ones grieving, but in it is the seed of our eventual recovery.

III. Has this realization ever struck us in time of grief? If so, how did we respond to it?

8. In time, grief diminishes as we resume our normal activities.

> **Genesis 38:12** Many days passing, Suah's daughter, Judah's wife, died. Taking consolation after grief, he went up to his sheep's shearers, he and *the* Adullamite Hiras, shepherd of *his* flock in Thamnas.

I. The next person who grieves, Judah, shows one way consolation comes in grief's aftermath. After an appropriate amount of time, Judah returns to his normal life.

II. How long does it take to resume our "normal activities" when grief strikes?

9. Anticipatory grief begins with Jacob, for Benjamin

> **Genesis 42:38:** [Jacob] said, "My son will not go down with you. His brother is dead and he only is left. If something bad happens to him in *the* land to which you bring him, you will lead my gray hairs down to *the* dead with grief."

I. This instance shows that anticipatory grief can be powerful. Jacob refuses to send his youngest son, Benjamin, to Egypt in care of his oldest son, Reuben, even though doing so puts the entire family at risk from the famine.

II. Jacob by this point in the story has good reason to distrust his eldest son, Reuben. Nevertheless, dysfunction in families often serves to intensify grief. How do we address this?

10. Judah, anticipating his father's grief over Benjamin, offers himself in his younger brother's place, and Pharaoh is moved to kindness.

> **Genesis 44:29:** If you take him too and something happens to him on *the* way, you will lead my gray hairs to *the* dead with grief.

I. In the next mention of grief, Judah recounts Jacob's words about Benjamin to Joseph (whom Judah has not recognized), and offers himself in Benjamin's place.
II. This is the first instance of a transformed heart (Judah), changed in this instance through suffering and grief.
III. The kind-hearted are mindful of the things that grieve others. Has this ever happened to you, or to someone you know?

11. Egypt and Israel grieve openly for Joseph.

> **Genesis 50:10-11:** They came to Atad's threshing floor, which was located across *the* Jordan, where they filled seven days celebrating funeral rights with great and severe grief. **50:11** When *the* inhabitants of Canaan's land had seen that, they said, "This great grief is to *the* Egyptians." Therefore, they call that place's name "Egypt's Grief."

I. This is the first instance of national, communal grief in scripture.
II. The final instance of grief in Genesis shows that grief impacts not merely individuals and families, but even nations, as the Egyptians alongside Jacob's descendants grieve the great Joseph following his death.
III. Grief can be public, powerful, clearly visible to others. When have you experienced this?

12. Nadab and Abiu's deaths highlight the grief that arises from our disobedience to God's commands.

> **Leviticus 10:6** Moses said to Aaron and to Eleazar and Ithamar his sons, "Don't uncover your heads and don't tear your garments, unless perhaps you die, and indignation rise over all *the* assembly! Let your brothers and all Israel's house grieve over *the* fire which *the* Lord aroused!

I. Nadab and Abiu, Aaron's sons, Moses' nephews, die in the midst of their ordination as priests after taking it upon themselves to change the rite that the Lord commanded.

II. Grief that arises from our disobedience to God's commands is stunted, and must be shunted on to others. After Nadab and Abiu sinned, Aaron and his surviving sons were forbidden to express their grief because of where they were, who they were, and what they were involved in. All Israel instead was forced to grieve in their place.

III. Have we ever experienced grief that arose from disobedience to the Lord?

13. Aaron's experience demonstrates the way grief interferes with our everyday activities.

> **Leviticus 10:19-20** Aaron answered, "*The* victim for sin was offered today and *the* burnt offering before *the* Lord. But you saw what happened to me. How could I eat or please *the* Lord in *the* ceremonies with *a* grieving mind?" **10:20** When Moses heard that, he accepted satisfaction.

I. Aaron acknowledges his grief over the loss, and Moses understands it.

II. When we are grieving over disobedience, we cannot please the Lord.

III. Grief interferes with our everyday activities, whether we want it to or not. How have we experienced this?

Grief Relief from the Bible, 20

14. Israel grieves at God's rebuke.

> **Numbers 14:39** Moses spoke all these words to all Israel's children, and *the* people grieved overwhelmingly.

I. The people, ordered by the Lord to take possession of the Promised Land after the Exodus, sent spies instead who came back with a discouraging report. At that point, Israel refused to obey the Lord's command to go to Canaan. Then, having been rebuked for disbelief, they grieved over the judgment that the Lord pronounces against them.

II. Sometimes our grief is too little, too late, when we have strayed from what God commands us. Have we ever experienced this?

15. Obedience to God's command takes precedence even over grief.

Deuteronomy 26:14 I have not eaten from it in my grief, or divided it in whatever uncleanness, or spent anything from it in *a* matter of funeral rites. I obeyed *the* Lord my God's voice, and did all that You commanded me.

I. This text concerns the Lord's command to Israel to bring the annual tithe to the nation's central place of worship.
II. Obedience to the Lord takes precedence even over our grief. Not even grief excuses us from following what the Lord commands.
III. How does faithfulness to the Lord keep our grief in perspective?

16. The Lord foresees the grief that will come to Israel when its faithlessness leads to exile.

Deuteronomy 28:65 Likewise, you will not be quiet among those nations, nor will your footsteps be in peace. *The* Lord will give you there *a* fearful heart and failing eyes and *a* soul consumed by grief.

I. The Lord warns Israel that they will grieve if they turn away from Him.
II. Grief will consume our souls when we are disobedient to the Lord.
III. One key to managing our grief is being in right relationship with our Creator. Do you feel like you are in right relationship with God now? If not, is it important to you to be so? How can you regain that relationship?

17. Israel grieves thirty days for Moses.

Deuteronomy 34:8 Israel's children wept for him thirty days in Moab's plains. Days of wailing and grieving were completed for Moses.

I. Israel grieved over Moses, as Egypt had wept over Joseph before them.
II. Even godly people and nations grieve.
III. What benefit does national grief offer a people?

18. Anna shares her grief before the Lord in earnest prayer, and gently turns away a false assumption about herself from Eli.

> **1 Samuel 1:16** Don't consider your handmade like one of Belial's daughters, because I've spoken from *the* multitude of my pains and griefs even to *the* present!"

I. Anna, speaking to the High Priest Eli at the Tent of Meeting in Shiloh, expresses her grief before God. Anna prayed silently, yet her lips were moving. Eli, watching her, believed she was drunk and rebuked her for it. She objected gently, and he blessed her.

II. Afterwards, because of her persistence in prayer and her straightforwardness toward Eli, the Lord gives Anna what she longs for, and eases her grief.

III. Has anyone ever misunderstood your grief? Have you ever misunderstood someone else's?

19. David and his companions grieve the deaths of Saul and Jonathan.

> **2 Samuel 1:12** They grieved and wept and fasted even to evening over Saul and over Jonathan his son and over *the* Lord's people and over Israel's house, because they had fallen by *the* sword.

I. David and his companions, in Ziklag, react to hearing news of the deaths of Saul and Jonathan in battle on Mount Gilboa at the hands of the Philistines. David and his companions grieve their deaths, despite Saul's repeated attempts to kill both David and his companions.

II. Do we ever grieve over those who seem to hate us? Why?

20. David expresses grief powerfully through music and lyrics.

> **2 Samuel 1:26** I grieve over you,
> my brother Jonathan –
> overwhelmingly handsome,
> and more worthy of love
> than *the* love of women.
> **1:27** How have *the* strong fallen,
> and *the* arms of war perished?

I. David grieved over Jonathan, his dear friend, through a Psalm.

II. Sometimes expressing grief through music can be healing. This is why we often sing and play music at funerals.

III. What kind of music helps you with grief?

21. David and his family grieve the murder of his eldest son by a younger brother, Absalom.

> **2 Samuel 13:36** When he stopped speaking, *the* king's sons appeared. Coming in, they lifted up their voice and wept. *The* king and all his slaves wept, too, with *an* overwhelmingly great grief.

I. Absalom himself was avenging the rape of his sister, Tamar, by Amnon, the king's first born son, whom Absalom killed.

II. Turmoil in families causes grief far beyond the initial causes.

III. Has this sort of grief over family turmoil ever touched your life? How can we respond to it?

22. Joab misuses a woman's pretended grief to manipulate David into an unwarranted act of pardon.

> **2 Samuel 14:1** Joab, Sarviah's son, understanding that *the* king's heart turned toward Absalom, **14:2** sent to Tekoa and took *a* wise woman from there. He said to her, "Act like you are grieving, and dress in grief's clothing. Don't be anointed with oil, so you may be like *a* woman already mourning *the* dead for *a* long time! **14:3** You will go into *the* king and speak such words to him."

I. Joab uses pretended grief to manipulate David into recalling Absalom from exile. The move has terrible consequences, as Absalom subsequently leads a rebellion against David.
II. Deceit and manipulation are a bad combination with grief, because of our vulnerability to them. Has this ever impacted you?

23. Joab rebukes David for grieving a son killed fighting against him.

> **2 Samuel 19:1** It was told to Joab that *the* king wept and mourned his son. **19:2** Victory was turned on that day into mourning for all *the* people, for *the* people heard it said on that day, "*The* king grieves over his son."

I. David grieved the death of his son, Absalom, in battle.
II. Absalom was killed after attempting to overthrow and kill his father.
III. Parents grieve their children, even when those children are irreconcilable and alienated.
IV. How can we deal with such grief?

Grief in Isaiah

24. Jerusalem's gates themselves will grieve the events coming upon the city.

> **Isaiah 3:26** Its gates will sorrow and grieve, and it will sit desolate on *the* ground.

I. Isaiah foresees Jerusalem's impending grief.
II. Do you foresee grief in the future? Is planning for grief morbid, or can it be freeing?

25. Isaiah sees Moab's upcoming grief over violent conquest.

> **Isaiah 15:1-4:** Because Ar was devastated by night, Moab fell silent. Because *the* wall was devastated by night, Moab fell silent. **15:2** *The* house went up, and Dibon to *the* high places, in grief over Nabo and over Medaba. Moab wailed in all its divisions. Every beard will be shaved to baldness. **15:3** They are girded in sackcloth in its crossroads. Each one wails on its roofs and in its streets. *Each* comes down in weeping. **15:4** Heshbon shouted, and Elealeh. Their voice was heard even to Iasa. Over this, Moab's soldiers will wail. Its soul will wail to itself.

I. Moab, a people living to Israel's east, was about to be conquered by the brutal Assyrian army.
II. Isaiah described Moab's grief and, in so doing, casts light on ancient processes of grieving.
III. How would we describe our process of grieving, and why do we do such things? How important is ritual to our coping and recovering from loss?

26. Isaiah himself weeps over Iazer's grief, as the cities across the Jordan River are plundered.

> **Isaiah 16:9** I will weep over this in Iazer's grief, Sabama's vineyard. I will make you drunk by my tears, Heshbon and Elealeh, because *the* tramplers' voice has rushed in over your grape-gathering and over your harvest.

I. Iazer, a city across the Jordan river to the east of Israel in Gilead, had long been fought over by the various kinglets of the region.
II. Now, Isaiah shares its grief as the Assyrians overrun and destroy it.
III. We grieve sometimes for the suffering of people we don't even know. Why? Is this healthy?

27. The working people of Egypt grieve as their livelihood dries up before them.

> **Isaiah 19:8** Fishermen will mourn, and all casting *a* hook in *the* river will grieve. *Those* throwing *a* net over water's face will grow weak. **19:9** *Those* who worked in linen, combing and spinning fine embroideries, will be confounded. **19:10** His irrigated *channels* will be failing, all who made hollows for capturing fish.

I. Egypt's farmers and fishermen lived by the annual floods of the Nile river. As those floods diminished, the laborers faced the prospect of famine and hunger.

II. It's easy to underestimate when things are going well for us how grievous economic setbacks can be. Has this ever impacted us?

28. Ariel, the city David built, grieves as it is besieged.

> **Isaiah 29:1** Woe, Ariel, Ariel, city which David built around! Year was added to year. Solemnities rolled around. **29:2** I will besiege Ariel, and it will be sad and grieving. It will be to Me like Ariel.

I. Ariel is another name for Jerusalem.

II. Isaiah foresees its grief as it is besieged by the Assyrian army.

III. What grief do you foresee in your life?

29. Merciless grief comes on the faithless.

> **Isaiah 51:19** *There* are two who have met you. Who will be sad over you – devastation, or grief, or hunger, or sword? Who will console you?

I. Isaiah sees in this vision the upcoming calamity Jerusalem eventually suffered at the hands of the Babylonians.

II. Yet he also foresees that the Lord will restore the city and the people, after their repentance.

III. What is our hope and consolation in grief if we don't believe in any life larger than ourselves?

30. The Lord calls one who was abandoned and grieving.

> **Isaiah 54:6** *The* Lord has called you, *you* who *were an* abandoned woman and *a* grieving breath, *a* wife rejected from youth, your God says.

I. Sometimes we grieve because others reject us. Yet in this passage, the Lord calls one who was abandoned.
II. Can it be that experiencing rejection is a necessary prelude to being redeemed?

31. The Lord brings Israel back from exile, and consoles those who grieved over Israel.

> **Isaiah 57:18** I saw his ways and forgave him. I brought him back, and repaid consolations to him and to those grieving for him.

I. Isaiah again sees the way that repentance, turning to the Lord, leads us beyond grief to restoration.
II. Have we ever experienced peace after turning toward the Lord? Why do you suppose some resist it so strongly?

32. When the Lord buys us back and becomes our everlasting light, grief can be completed,

> **Isaiah 60:20** Your sun will set no more, and your moon will not be diminished, for *the* Lord will be as everlasting light, and *the* days of your grief will be completed.

I. In this vision of restoration and redemption, Isaiah holds forth the insight that grief can come to an end by the Lord's mercy and redemption.
II. How important is it to hold on to this hope when we are grieving? How best can we do so?

33. The Lord appoints Sion to the grieving.

> **Isaiah 61:1** *The* Lord's breath is on me, because *the* Lord has anointed me to preach to *the* gentle. He sent me to heal *the* shattered in heart, that I might proclaim pardon to *the* captive, and opening to *the* closed in; **61:2** that I might proclaim *the* year of *the* Lord's appeasing, and *the* day of vengeance to our God, that I might console all *the* grieving; **61:3** that I might appoint Sion to *the* grieving, and give them *a* crown for ashes, joy's oil for weeping, praise's covering for *a* mourning breath. They will be called mighty *ones* of righteousness in it, *the* Lord's planting, to glorifying.

I. Sion (or Zion) is another name for Jerusalem. Here, though, it stands not merely for the earthly city, but the divine home God provides for those He redeems from grief.
II. Scripture clearly teaches that there is a better world ahead for those who trust God. Do we believe this? Is it helpful to us?

34. Those who grieve over Jerusalem are invited to rejoice over her.

> **Isaiah 66:10** Rejoice with Jerusalem, and exult in her all who love her! Be joyful with her in joy, all you who grieve over her, **66:11** that you nurse and be filled again from her consolation's breast, that you may drink milk and abound in delights from every mode of her glory!

I. Sometimes when others recover from grief, those who love them also rejoice. Has this ever happened to you?

Grief Relief from the Bible, 29

35. Earth and sky will grieve when the Lord judges in righteousness.

> **Jeremiah 4:28** *The* land will mourn and skies above will grieve, because I have spoken. I considered, and it did not displease Me, nor have I turned back from it.

I. Jeremiah implies that the creation itself grieves when the Lord judges human wickedness.
II. Can this be true, or is it merely poetic language?

36. Jeremiah urges the people to grieve over the coming destruction as if over a firstborn child.

> **Jeremiah 6:26** Wrap yourself in rough clothing, my people's daughter, and sprinkle *yourselves* with ashes! Make yourselves *a* bitter wail for grief *over a* firstborn, for *the* destroyer will come quickly over us!

I. Few griefs compare to the loss of a firstborn child.
II. Jeremiah warns the people to grieve that way, as judgment comes over them from God. Why?

37. The prophet's heart grieves as the people realizes its acts have resulted in the Lord abandoning their cherished places.

> **Jeremiah 8:18** My pain *is* beyond pain. My heart *is* grieving within me. **8:19** Look! *The* voice of my people's daughter, shouting from *a* faraway land, "Is *the* Lord not in Sion, or is His king not in her?"

I. Sometimes, we realize just how far our actions have led us from the God who is our hope and consolation.
II. Here, the Jewish exiles grieve, realizing the Lord has abandoned the holy city of Jerusalem.
III. Have you ever lost something you considered holy? How did it impact you?

38. Jeremiah urges the women of Judah to learn to grieve, in light of the coming catastrophe.

> **Jeremiah 9:20** Listen then, women, to *the* Lord's word, and let your ear take up His mouth's word! Teach your daughters *the* lament, and *let* each one *teach* grief to her neighbor! **9:21** Death climbs up through our windows! It has come into our houses to kill *the* little ones from outside, *the* youth from *the* broad streets.

I. **Jeremiah's exhortation to Judah's women** to grieve over the coming fury gives an insight to the way that we humans learn to grieve culturally from those around us. (Note that all references to Judah from here forward are to the tribe and nation, not to the individual).

II. **Who is teaching you** how to grieve? What lessons are you learning?

39. The prophet grieves having been born to witness the unfolding catastrophe, in which God will destroy Judah "without grief."

> **Jeremiah 20:14** *Let the* day *be* cursed when I was born! Let *the* day when my mother birthed me not be blessed! **20:15** *Let the* man *be* cursed who told my father, saying, "*A* boy child is born to you," and made him happy as if by joy! **20:16** Let that man be like *the* cities which *the* Lord overthrew, and it did not grieve Him. Let him hear *a* cry at morning, and wailing at midday **20:17** who did not kill me from *the* vulva, that my mother might be my grave and her vulva *an* eternal home!

I. **Some events in life** can be so painful that they cause us to regret ever being born.

II. **Have you ever** experienced that? If so, how do we recover from that?

40. Jeremiah urges Israel not to cause grief to strangers, as part of its turning back to the Lord.

> **Jeremiah 22:3** *The* Lord says this: Work judgment and righteousness! Free one pushed down by violence from *the* oppressor's hand! Don't grieve newcomer and orphan and widow, or oppress treacherously! Don't pour out innocent blood in this place! **22:4** If you will surely work this word, kings of David's line will go in through *the* gates of this house, sitting on his throne and mounting chariots with their horses and slaves, and *the* people will serve.

I. **Judah's abuse of strangers and travelers** is one of the reasons the Lord judged His people.

II. **When our actions grieve others,** that grief often rebounds on our own heads.

III. **Have we ever experienced that?** What lesson does that teach us?

41. Some conditions in life are more grievous than death.

> **Jeremiah 22:10** Don't weep over *the* dead, or grieve over him! Mourn with tears over him who goes out, because he will not return further, nor see his native land!

I. For a people raised from childhood to believe that the land they inhabited had been given them by God, losing that land forever was worse in their eyes than dying.
II. What things or places do you love more than life itself?

42. Jeremiah is heart-sick at the Israelites' wickedness to each other, and even the land where it lives grieves at the sin.

> **Jeremiah 23:9** My heart is broken toward *the* prophets. All my bones trembled together within me. I became like *a* drunken man and like *a* man sodden with wine, before *the* Lord's face and before *the* face of His holy words – **23:10** because *the* land is full of adulterers, because *the* land grieves before cursing's face. Abandoned fields have dried up. Their course has become harm and their strength *a* lie.

I. Jeremiah suffers godly grief at the cruelty and unfaithfulness of those who are supposed to be God's people.
II. Has the hypocrisy of supposed believers ever grieved you? **Has your hypocrisy** as a believer ever grieved someone else?
III. How do we respond?

43. The Lord will restore a repentant Israel, and turn its grief into joy.

> **Jeremiah 31:13** Then, *the* virgin will rejoice in dance, youths and elders together, and I will turn their grief into joy. I will console them, and make them glad from their sorrow. **31:14** I will make *the* priest's soul drunk from fatness, and My people will be filled by My good *blessings*, *the* Lord said.

I. Despite the people's unfaithfulness, God remains faithful to them. The Lord will restore them when they are repentant.
II. Is this adequate consolation for the sufferings we endure?

44. The prophet hears the mothers of Israel grieving over their slain children.

> **Jeremiah 31:15** *The* Lord says this: *A* voice is heard on *the* height, lamentation's tears and grief, Rachel weeping her sons. She won't be consoled over them, because they are not.

I. This passage, spoken as Nebuchadnezzar carried the Jewish people away into exile, will be echoed in Matthew when murderous King Herod kills the infants of Bethlehem following Christ's birth.
II. Though the Lord will bring a terrible judgment on the heads of wicked rulers, those who are their victims nevertheless mourn.
III. What is the consolation of the victim before the one victimizing?

45. The Lord commands the people to cease grieving because their exiles will return.

> **Jeremiah 31:16** *The* Lord says this: Let your voice be quiet from weeping, and your eyes from tears, for *this* is *the* reward of your works, *the* Lord said. They will come back from *the* enemy's land. **31:17** This is hope for your ends, *the* Lord said, and sons will come back to your borders.

I. In the midst of the catastrophe of Jerusalem's destruction and the Jewish exile, the Lord promises that He is not through with His people. He will yet have mercy on them.
II. Do we sometimes give up on God during our grief, when He hasn't given up on us?

46. The prophet cries out against Moab, even as Moab grieves over its own judgment and destruction.

> **Jeremiah 48:31** Therefore, I will wail against Moab, and cry out to all Moab, to *the* grieving men of *the* clay wall. **48:32** I will weep over you, from Iazer's grief. Your cuttings, Sobema's vineyard, passed through *the* sea. They came through even to Iazer's sea. *The* plunderer rushed in against your harvest and your grape-gathering

I. Such had been Moab's cruelty and treachery toward Jerusalem that Jeremiah continued to denounce them, even as Moab suffered grievous harm from the Assyrians.
II. Can others so wrong us that we do not feel sadness even over their grief? Can that be resolved?

47. Every grief has come upon Moab as the Lord destroys it for its sin.

> **Jeremiah 48:38** Every grief *is* over all Moab's roofs and in its streets, because I have shattered Moab like *a* useless vessel, *the* Lord said.

I. The nation that played both sides against the middle suffers utter destruction from the Lord's judgment.
II. Every type of grief comes upon Moab as it falls before the Assyrians.
III. How do we balance the desire for revenge with mercy toward those who suffer?

Grief Relief from the Bible, 34

48. Ezekiel grieves for seven days among the exiles after his vision of the Lord's glory, yet his grief is prelude to his service as prophet.

> **Ezekiel 3:15** I went to *the* captives, to *the* heap of new crops, to those who live beside *the* Chobar river, and I sat where they sat. I rested there seven days, grieving among them. **3:16** When seven days had passed, *the* Lord's word came to me, saying, **3:17** "Man's son, I have given you as *a* scout to Israel's house. You will hear *the* word from My mouth, and you will tell them from Me.

I. Ezekiel was one of the Jewish captives carried away by the Baylonians.
II. He is given a vision of God in exile, outside the Promised Land, something most believed was impossible. Though the vision grieved him, it marked the beginning of his career as the Lord's prophet.
III. Can grief be the beginning (or deepening) of our walk with the Lord?

49. Even the most powerful in Jerusalem will grieve as the consequences of their disobedience unfold.

> **Ezekiel 7:26** "Trouble over trouble will come, and rumor over rumor. They will seek vision from *a* prophet. Law will perish from *the* priest, and counsel from *the* elders. **7:27** *The* king will mourn, and *the* prince will be dressed in grieving. *The* hands of *the* land's people will be troubled. I will do to them according to their way. I will judge them according to their judgments, and they will know that I *am the* Lord."

I. Wealth and power can buy us many things, but they cannot buy us an exemption from grief.
II. What things that we believe to be assets to us might become liabilities when grief comes? How should we respond?

50. The prophet, carried into the Temple by an angel, sees Israelite women grieving over the pagan god Adonis, a misdirected grief leading to their judgment by the Lord.

> **Ezekiel 8:14** He brought me through *the* door of *the* gate of *the* Lord's house that looked to *the* north, and look! Women were sitting, grieving for Adonis! **8:15** He said to me, "Certainly you have seen, man's son. Turning still, you will see worse abominations than these."

I. The worship of false gods turned the people away from the Lord, and set the stage for their grief.
II. Do we or those around us worship false gods? Where does this happen, and where does it lead?

51. The Lord commands the prophet to eat bread and drink water while grieving, as a prophetic model for the exiles of the situation of those left behind in Jerusalem.

> **Ezekiel 12:17** *The* Lord's word came to me, saying, **12:18** "Man's son, eat your bread in trouble, yet also drink your water in hurrying and grieving. **12:19** You will say to *the* land's people, *The* Lord God says this to those who live in Jerusalem, in Israel's land: They will eat their bread in worry, and drink their water in desolation, so *the* land may be abandoned by its multitude – because of *the* iniquity of all who live in it. **12:20** Cities that now are inhabited will be abandoned and *the* land deserted, and you will know that I *am the* Lord.

I. As often happened in Ezekiel's career as prophet, the Lord called him to act out a visual parable for his fellow exiles, modeling the grief coming upon Jerusalem.

II. Why does seeing someone's grief impact us more powerfully than merely being told about it? How has this impacted you?

52. The Lord rebukes false prophets who have made righteous people grieve over issues that warranted no grieving, and promises to rescue the righteous from the liars' hands.

> **Ezekiel 13:22** "Because you've made *a* righteous heart grieve falsely whom I have not saddened, and you've strengthened *a* lawless hand that it not turn back from its harmful way and live, **13:23** therefore, you will see vanity and foretell guesses no longer. I will rescue My people from your hand, and you will know that I am *the* Lord."

I. The Lord rebukes those who have deceived His faithful ones, promising both to judge the self-appointed prophets and to save those they have grieved.

II. What would constitute making a "righteous heart grieve falsely" today? How would that impact our grief?

53. Judah will drink a cup of grieving for having followed the malign example of her sister Israel.

> **Ezekiel 23:32** *The* Lord God says this: "You will drink your sister's cup, deep and wide. You will be in derision and in mocking, *of* which you are most fitting. **23:33** You will be filled with drunkenness and pain, *a* cup of grieving and sadness, *the* cup of Samaria your sister. **23:34** You will drink it, and suck it down even to *the* dregs. You will devour its fragments and tear your breasts, because I have spoken," *the* Lord God said.

I. Judah (centered on Jerusalem) and Israel (centered finally on Samaria) were the two Hebrew statelets left after the collapse of Solomon's empire under his son Rehoboam. Rehoboam, famously, took terrible advice.

II. Sometimes the role models we follow lead us to grief.

III. How do we tell which models to follow and which to reject?

54. Ezekiel is commanded not to publicly grieve the death of his wife, as a portent and example to the Jewish exiles.

> **Ezekiel 24:15** *The* Lord's word came to me, saying, **24:16** "Man's son, look! I am taking *the* desire of your eyes away from you at *a* blow, and you will neither mourn, nor weep, nor will your tears flow. **24:17** Groan silently! You will not work *the* grief of *the* dead. Let your crown be tied around your *head*, and your shoes will be on your feet – nor will you cover your mouth with *a* veil, nor will you eat *the* food of *the* grieving." **24:18** I spoke to *the* people at morning, therefore, and my wife died at evening. I did at morning as He commanded Me. **24:19** *The* people said to me, "Why don't you tell us what these *things* mean that you are doing?" **24:20** I said to them, "*The* Lord's word came to me, saying, **24:21** Say to Israel's house, *The* Lord God says this: Look! I will pollute My sanctuary, your power's pride and your eyes' desire, over which your soul fears. Your sons and daughters whom you left behind will fall by *the* sword.' **24:22** "You will do as I did. You will not cover your mouth with *a* veil, and you will not eat *the* food of *the* grieving. **24:23** You will have crowns on your heads and shoes on your feet. You will not grieve or weep, yet you will waste away in your iniquities. Each one will moan to his brother. **24:24** Ezekiel will be to you as *a* portent. You will do according to all that he did when this has come, and you will know that I *am the* Lord. **24:25** "You, man's son, look! On *the* day when I take away from them their strength and dignity's joy and their eyes' desire on which their souls rest, their sons and daughters, **24:26** on that day, when *the* one fleeing comes to you so he may tell you, **24:27** on that day, I say, your mouth will be opened with him who flees. You will speak and be silent no further. You will be to them as *a* portent, and you will know that I *am the* Lord."

I. Ezekiel's contemporaries considered it a sacred obligation to grieve the loss of loved ones. In this instance the Lord specifically commands Ezekiel not to publicly grieve the death of his beloved wife, as an example to the people.
II. Are there times of such hardship that we can't even find the opportunity to grieve? What happens when those times pass?

55. God will punish the Palestinians for their violence over ancient grievances.

> **Ezekiel 25:15** *The* Lord God says this: "Because *the* Palestinians worked in vengeance, and avenged themselves with all *the* soul, killing and fulfilling ancient grievances, **25:16** for this reason, *the* Lord God says this: look! I will stretch out My hand over *the* Palestinians. I will kill *the* killers, and destroy *the* survivors of *the* seaside regions. **25:17** I will work great vengeance among them, rebuking in fury, and they will know that I *am the* Lord, when I give My revenge over them."

I. Because the Palestinians could not find it in their hearts to let go of ancient grievances, their thirst for revenge will merely bring greater pain on themselves.
II. How important is it in our grieving that we learn to forgive?

56. Those who grew rich trading with Tyre will grieve over its fall.

> **Ezekiel 27:32** "They will take up *a* mournful song over you, and grieve over you. Who is like Tyre, who is silent in *the* sea's midst...

I. Tyre was a wealthy seaport in Lebanon, which was captured and destroyed by Nebuchadnezzar.
II. Sometimes our deepest grief is over people or things that once gave us pleasure, but can do so no longer.
III. Have you ever experienced this? Is such grief misdirected?

57. Ezekiel himself is commanded by the Lord to grieve over Tyre.

> **Ezekiel 28:11** *The* Lord's word came to me, saying, "Man's son, lift up grief over Tyre's king! **28:12** You will say to him, *The* Lord God says this: You *were a* sign like *one* full of wisdom and perfect in beauty.

I. Despite Tyre's pagan roots, Ezekiel receives instruction to grieve over it.
II. Our human compassion should not be limited only to those who share our faith.
III. How ought we grieve over those who differ greatly from us?

58. Even the skies above will grieve over Pharaoh's destruction.

> **Ezekiel 32:7** "I will cover *the* skies when you are extinct, and make its stars darken. I will cover *the* sun with cloud, and *the* moon will not give its light. **32:8** I will make all *the* sky's lights grieve over you, and place shadows over your land," *the* Lord God says.

I. The destruction of Pharaoh's regime at the hand of the Babylonians was an unprecedented event in the ancient world. Egypt seemed to have been immune from invasion because of the impassable deserts on its borders. Nebuchadnezzar showed the world this was not the case.
II. Some events in our world are so profound that they seem to grieve even the natural world itself. Can you imagine such an event? Have you ever experienced such?

Grief in Hosea

59. Ephraim in its hardness of heart does not know how to grieve unto repentance.

> **Hosea 13:11** "I will give you *a* king in my fury, and will take *him* away in my indignation. **13:12** Ephraim's iniquity is bound up. His sin *is* hidden. **13:13** Labor pains will come on him. He *is a* child *who* doesn't understand, for now he will not stand in *the* children's grief.

I. Hosea was called as a prophet to the northern kingdom of Israel, called Ephraim here after the name of its largest tribe. The northern Israelite tribes had rebelled against the Davidic kingdom in Jerusalem, after the death of Solomon.
II. Because Israel refuses the Lord's exhortation to repent, grief will come upon it. Do we suffer similarly when we refuse to turn to the Lord?

60. God will heal Israel's grief after the nation turns back to Him.

> **Hosea 14:5** "I will heal their griefs. I will love them willingly, because My fury has turned back from him.

I. Despite the people's rebellion, the Lord loves them and will heal their grief.
II. Is this promise still true? Is it helpful in grief?

Grief Relief from the Bible, 39

61. The prophet calls Israel to mourn over the coming disaster, noting that even the priests have grieved.

> **Joel 1:8** Wail like *a* virgin wearing mourning clothes over *the* husband of her youth! **1:9** Sacrifice and drink offering have ceased from *the* Lord's house. Priests, *the* Lord's ministers, have grieved.

I. Joel arises as a prophet to warn the people over a plague of destroying insects devastating their country. He urges the people to sincere repentance.
II. Did Israel's repentance cause the plague of locusts to diminish? If not, was there any value in it?
III. Can repentance turn away grief?

Grief Relief from the Bible, 40

62. The prophet rebukes the rich among the people, who have not grieved over the calamity coming on Joseph's descendants.

> **Amos 6:1** Woe to you who are in luxury on Sion and who trust in Samaria's mountain – nobles, *the* peoples' heads, going in with pomp to Israel's house! **6:2** Go to Chalanne and see! Go from there to great Emath, and go down into *the* Palestinians' Gath, and to *the* best of their kingdoms! *See* if their border was wider than your border – **6:3** *you* who are set apart to *the* harmful day, and come close to iniquity's throne; **6:4** who sleep in ivory beds and lust in your bedrooms, who eat lamb from *the* flock and calves from *the* herd's midst; **6:5** who sing to *the* stringed instrument's voice. You considered yourselves to have musical instruments like David, **6:6** drinking wine in drinking plates and thickly smeared with *the* best ointment. Yet they suffered nothing over Joseph's grief.

I. Amos, a humble agricultural worker from Judah called by the Lord to prophesy to the northern kingdom of Israel, reminds them that their riches and power do not make them immune to grief.
II. Do we sometimes trust in our possessions more than in the Lord? Where does this lead?

63. When the Lord visits on Israel the consequences of its actions, the nation will grieve.

> **Amos 8:7** *The* Lord has sworn against Jacob's pride, "Will I forget all their works even to *the* end? **8:8** Won't *the* land be moved over this, and each of its inhabitants grieve? Won't it rise like *an* all-covering flood, and cast out and wash away like Egypt's river? **8:9** *It* will be in that day, *the* Lord says, sun will set at midday, and I will make *the* land shadow over in daylight. **8:10** I will turn your festivities into grief, and all your music into wailing. I will put sackcloth on every back, and baldness on every head. I will make her like firstborn grief, and his end like *a* bitter day."

I. Amos reminds prosperous Israel that sooner or later, the Lord will bring a grievous judgment against sin.
II. Have our "festivities" ever turned "into grief"? When, and how so? What lessons does that teach us?

Grief Relief from the Bible, 41

64. The Lord rebukes Jonah for grieving for ivy, yet not grieving for Nineveh in its sin.

Jonah 4:10 *The* Lord said, "You grieve over ivy, for which you didn't labor, and neither did you work to make it grow – which was born under one night and died *the* next night! **4:11** Will I not spare Nineveh, *a* great city where are more than *a* hundred twenty thousand men who do not know what may be between their right and left, and many cattle?"

I. Jonah hates Nineveh, capital of the cruel Assyrian empire that had devastated his country. He resists God's call to preach to it, trying instead to escape. When he does preach and Nineveh actually repents, Jonah grieves more over a plant that gave him shade than over a people who had almost been destroyed.
II. Does our hatred make it impossible to grieve for our enemies?

Grief Relief from the Bible, 42

Grief in Micah

65. The prophet will be filled with wild grief at the calamity coming upon Judah.

> **Micah 1:8** I will lament and wail. I will go robbed and naked. I will make *a* lament like dragons and grief like ostriches, **1:9** because its wound is desperate, because it came even to Judah. It has touched my people's gate, even to Jerusalem.

I. Micah, who prophesied to Judah during the 8th Century BC, sees God's judgment coming upon his nation, and grieves over it.

II. Have we ever experienced a calamity coming upon ourselves, our families, or our communities? How did we respond?

66. The Lord questions ironically why Judah grieves, since all the things it has trusted instead of God are still in place.

> **Micah 4:9** Now, why are you depressed by grief? Is *the* king not with you? Has your counselor perished because pain overtakes you like one giving birth? **4:10** Suffer and be hard-pressed, Sion's daughter, like one giving birth! Now you will go out from *the* city, and live in *the* region, and come even to Babylon. There you will be freed. There *the* Lord will buy you back from your enemies' hands.

I. The Lord seems to mock Judah through the prophet. Though the things Judah trusts are still intact, the people nevertheless grieves.

II. What happens when the things we trust do not help us? How ought we to respond?

Grief Relief from the Bible, 43

67. Assyria's grief is not hidden as it receives the just deserts of its crimes.

Nahum 3:18 Your shepherds slept, Assyria's King. Your princes will be buried. Your people has hidden itself in *the* mountains, and *there* is no one who will come together. **3:19** Your grief is not hidden. Your wound is dismal. All who heard your report clenched *a* fist over you, because over whom has your harmful way not passed?"

I. The prophet Nahum sees God's judgment coming upon Nineveh, capital of Assyria, despite its apparent power.
II. Again, we see that power and wealth do not insulate us from grief, and that God eventually punishes iniquity.
III. Does that still happen? If it does, would it touch us? How ought we to respond?

Grief Relief from the Bible, 44

Grief in Habakkuk

68. The Lord announces to Babylon that its grief will be harsh, after it has plundered many nations.

Habakkuk 2:6 "Won't all of them take up *a* parable over him and his cryptic speech? It will be said, 'Woe to him who multiplies what isn't his. How long also harsh grief weighs down against him!' **2:7** Won't those who bite you rise up quickly? Those tearing you will be aroused, and you will be like plunder to them.

I. Habakkuk, a contemporary of Daniel, sees God's judgment coming upon the Babylonian empire that had destroyed Jerusalem and taken its people into exile.
II. If we will receive back from others the griefs we have given them, how ought we to live?

Grief Relief from the Bible, 45

69. The Lord tells the people that its religious grief was insincere and self-centered, bringing about change neither in the people's hearts nor in the Lord.

> **Zechariah 7:4** *The* Lord of armies' word came to me, saying, **7:5** "Speak to all *the* land's people, and to *the* priests, saying, when you fasted and grieved in *the* fifth and seventh months through those seventy years, you didn't fast your fast to Me, did you? **7:6** When you ate and when you drank, didn't you eat for yourselves and also drink for yourselves?

I. Zechariah prophesied to the Jewish people after their exile in Babylon. That fact that he prophesied made evident the fulfillment of what God had promised through Isaiah and Jeremiah: that the people would survive exile and return to Jerusalem.

II. The Lord through the prophet rebukes the people's self-centered religious expression. Do we have a "religious expression"? If so, is it God-centered, or is it centered on us? Does it matter?

70. Israel will grieve over the slain Messiah, as people grieve over the death of firstborn children.

> **Zechariah 12:10** I will pour out *a* graceful and prayerful spirit over David's house and over Jerusalem's inhabitants, and they will look on Me whom they affixed with nails. They will lament with wailing as if over an only child. They will grieve over Him, as one is accustomed to grieve over *the* death of *a* firstborn child. **12:11** In that day, grief will be great in Jerusalem, like Adadremmon's grief in Megiddo's field. **12:12** *The* land will wail, families and families separately, and David's house separately, and their women separately – **12:13** *the* families of Nathan's house separately, and their women separately; *the* families of Levi's house separately, and their women separately; Shemei's families separately, and their women separately, **12:14** all *the* survivors' families, families and families separately, and their women separately.

I. Through Christian eyes, Zechariah seems to anticipate Christ's crucifixion, which happened several hundred years later.

II. The people will grieve again over the "pierced" Messiah, as if for a firstborn child. How does this impact us?

Grief Relief from the Bible, 46

71. The Lord has sent a desperate grief into Israel following the Babylonian destruction of Jerusalem.

> **Lamentations 1:13** MEM. He sent fire into my bones from *the* high *place*, and taught me. He stretched out *a* net for my feet. He turned me back. He set me desolate all day, reduced by grief.

I. Jeremiah, who survived the Babylonian destruction of Jerusalem, wrote the book of Lamentations in its aftermath.
II. He expresses poetic astonishment at the grief he suffers, even though he knew it was coming.
III. Does knowing grief is coming lessen it?

72. The prophet prays that Judah's plunderers may suffer, even as its people now grieve.

> **Lamentations 1:22** THAU. May all their harm come in before You! Strip their grapes from them also, as You've gathered mine, because of all my iniquities – for my groans *are* many, and my heart *is* grieving!

I. In his pain, Jeremiah prays that those who inflicted such grief on Jerusalem would suffer it in turn.
II. Jeremiah's prayer voices an honest, human response to violence and depredation. We acknowledge the desire for revenge, yet we have a choice of how we respond to it.
III. Again, how do we face the question of forgiveness in the process of grieving?

Grief Relief from the Bible, 47

73. Ezra grieves over how the Jews have polluted themselves by marrying outsiders.

Ezra 9:1 After these were finished, *the* princes came to me, saying, "Israel's people is not separated – and *the* priests, and *the* Levites – from *the* lands' peoples and from their abominations, *the* Canaanites, of course, and Hittites, and Ferezites, and Jebusites, and Ammanites, and Moabites, and Egyptians, and Amorites. **9:2** They took for themselves from their daughters and their sons, and they mixed holy seed with *the* lands' people. Even *the* princes' and magistrates' hand was first in this transgression." **9:3** When I heard this word, I tore my cloak and tunic, and tore out *the* hairs of my head and beard, and sat grieving. **9:4** All who feared *the* word of Israel's God concerning their transgression, who came from *the* captivity, came together to me, and I sat sorrowful even to *the* evening sacrifice.

I. Ezra is High Priest while the returning Jewish exiles rebuild Jerusalem. In the process of reestablishing the nation, the priesthood uncovers mixed marriages between Jews and non-Jews.

II. Though we may question Ezra's view of intermarriage, there is no denying that a marriage between two people may cause grief to others. How have we experienced this?

Grief Relief from the Bible, 48

74. Nehemiah tells the people not to grieve after hearing the law and realizing their shortcomings, because "the joy of the Lord is your strength."

> **Nehemiah 8:9** Nehemiah spoke (he is Athersatha), and Ezra *the* priest, *the* scribe, and *the* Levites, interpreting to all *the* people, "*The* day is sanctified to *the* Lord our God. Don't grieve and don't weep!" (For all *the* people wept when it heard *the* law's words.) **8:10** He said to them, "Go, eat fat *things*, and drink sweet wine! Send portions to him who has not prepared himself, because *the* Lord's day is holy! Don't be sad, for *the* joy of *the* Lord is our strength!" **8:11** *The* Levites made silence among all *the* people, saying, "Be quiet because *the* day is holy! Don't grieve!" **8:12** So all *the* people went out so it could eat, and drink, and send portions, and make *a* great joy, because they understood *the* words that he taught them.

I. The Jewish people, having returned from exile and hearing the law read as they rededicate the Temple, begin to grieve as they realize how short of it they have fallen.

II. Nehemiah, Ezra, and the leaders insist that they stop grieving and celebrate instead.

III. The "joy of the Lord", which manifests itself in pardon for our sin, transforms our grief. Have you ever experienced this?

Grief Relief from the Bible, 49

75. Haman grieves, realizing his wicked plot against Mordecai is rebounding on his own head.

> **Esther 6:12** Mordecai went back to *the* palace door, and Haman hurried to go to his *own* house, grieving and head covered. **6:13** He told Zares his wife and all his friends all that happened to him. *The* wise men whom he had in counsel and his wife answered him, "If Mordecai, before whom you've begun to fall, is from *the* Jews' seed, you won't be able to resist him – yet you will fall in his sight."

I. Haman the Amalekite is determined to destroy Mordecai and the Jews, in revenge for an ancient grievance. When his plans begin to go astray, he grieves the loss of his opportunity for revenge.
II. Do we ever grieve when we are unable to bring about harm to others?

76. Mordecai commands the Jews to celebrate as a festival the days when the Lord turned their grieving into joy.

> **Esther 9:20** So Mordecai wrote all these. Taking letters sent to *the* Jews who were living in all *the* king's provinces – both *those* placed nearby and *those* far away – **9:21** that they take *the* fourteenth and fifteenth day of *the* month of Adar as *a* festival, and they celebrate *the* solemnity with honor always, when *the* year turned, **9:22** because on that day, *the* Jews avenged themselves against their enemies, and grief and sadness were turned to cheerfulness and joy; and these might be days of feasting and joy, and they might send each other portions of food, and small presents might be granted to *the* poor.

I. The deliverance of the Jews from Haman's plot is an occasion of great joy, made more pronounced by the expectation of harm it replaced.
II. Have we ever experienced unexpected deliverance from grief?

Grief Relief from the Bible, 50

77. Eliphaz prays to the Lord, who turns grieving into joy.

(Spoken by Eliphaz)
Job 5:8 From which thing
I pray to *the* Lord,
and direct my eloquence to God...
5:11 who places *the* humble on high,
and raises *the* grieving to safety...

I. Eliphaz is one of three friends who visit Job after he suffers a series of calamities that leave him childless and destitute.
II. He urges Job to repent of what he imagines was the sin that caused his suffering, confident that the Lord can transform his grief. Job, though, insists he suffers innocently. Have we ever been in that position?

78. Job remembers that, despite the power and influence he once possessed, he still consoled the grieving.

(Spoken by Job)
Job 29:25 If I wanted to go to them,
I sat as leader,
and when I sat down,
I was like *a* king surrounded by *an* army –
yet I consoled *the* grieving.

I. Job, discussing his plight with his friends, remembers that during his prosperity and power, he nevertheless took time for those who grieved.
II. Do the powerful people we know of take time to comfort the grieving? Is that helpful?

79. Job acknowledges the grief that has risen up in him during his sufferings.

(Spoken by Job)
Job 30:27 My guts have boiled
up without any peace.
Days of affliction have come over me.
30:28 I walked along grieving,
without anger.
Rising up in *a* crowd I cried out.

I. Job's grief is so severe that his life is utterly without peace. He isn't angry. He's just hurting.
II. Have we or someone we know ever grieved so severely that all else seemed to disappear? How did we recover?

80. Job's family and friends come to him after the tragedy and grieve over him, sharing their wealth with him and participating in the restoration of his fortunes.

> **Job 42:10** *The* Lord was turned also to Job's penance when he had prayed for his friends, and *the* Lord added all that Job had possessed twice over. **42:11** All his brothers and all his sisters and all who knew him before came to him. They ate bread with him in his house, and grieved over him. They comforted him over all *the* harm which God had inflicted on him. Each one gave to him one sheep and one gold earring.

I. At the end of the book, Job's remaining family and friends come to console him.
II. They help restore his prosperity by sharing their material goods with him.
III. How can the help of loving friends and family ease our recovery from grief? What do we need from them? What lessons can we take from this when those we care about are the ones grieving?

Grief Relief from the Bible, 52

Grief in Proverbs

81. A foolish son causes his mother grief.

Proverbs 10:1 Parables of Solomon.
A wise son gives *a* father joy.
A foolish son, truly, is *a* grief to his mother.

I. Parents, perhaps especially mothers, suffer grief from the actions of their children.
II. Is this a grief we can ever recover from? If so, how so?

82. Lack of a trustworthy guide leads the people to grief.

Proverbs 11:14 Where
there is no guide,
the people come to grief.
Safety *is* where *there are* many counsels.

I. Nations grieve when wise leadership is absent.
II. How can citizens of a democracy work to insure wise leadership is rewarded?

83. When joy peters out, grief takes over.

Proverbs 14:13 Laughter
will be mixed with pain,
and grief takes over *the* end of joy.

I. It is unreasonable to expect a life where there is only laughter and joy.
II. How do our expectations about such things impact us when grief comes?

84. A grieving soul brings down a person's spirit.

> **Proverbs 15:13** *A* rejoicing heart
> gladdens *the* face.
> *The* spirit is brought down
> by *a* grieving soul.

I. Grief within us can't help but impact our entire life.
II. Are we sensitive to the impact of grief on our own lives, or on the lives of others?

85. Lemuel's mother counsels him to give strong drink to those who grieve.

> **Proverbs 31:6** Give
> strong drink to *the* grieving,
> and wine to those who are bitter in soul.
> **31:7** They may drink and forget their need,
> and not remember their pain *any* more.

I. There are times when grief is sufficiently severe as to need medication.
II. Can we bring ourselves to be gentle to ourselves and others in grief?
III. How do we feel about the role of medication in dealing with mental distress and anguish?

Grief Relief from the Bible, 54

Grief in Ecclesiastes

86. There is a time for grieving, as there is for all other eventualities in life.

Ecclesiastes 3:4 ...time for weeping
and time for laughing;
time for bitter grieving
and time to leap for joy...

I. No one in this world, not even the Lord, is exempt from grief.
II. How accepting are we of the inevitability of grief? Would we sacrifice our joy, if it meant not feeling grief?

Grief Relief from the Bible, 55

Grief in Psalms

87. The Psalmist humbled himself in grief for a companion, only to be betrayed by him.

> **Psalms 34:14** As if *a* neighbor,
> as if our brother,
> so I made myself acceptable.
> Like one weeping and grieved,
> so I humbled myself.

I. Sometimes when we grieve for others, they do not grieve for us in turn when we suffer hardship.
II. Should we withhold our grief over the pain others suffer until we find out whether they will return it?

88. The Lord Himself rescued the Psalmist from grief and restored his fortunes.

> **Psalms 39:3** He heard my prayers.
> He led me out of misery's pit
> and grief's dregs.
> He stood my feet on *a* rock
> and guided my steps.

I. The Psalmist rejoices that the Lord heard his prayer and restored him.
II. Have we experienced answers to our prayer? How does this impact our grieving?

89. The Psalmist prays the Lord to heal the land's grief, after the Lord had moved it.

> **Psalms 59:4** You moved *the* land
> and troubled it.
> Heal its grief, because it was moved!

I. This verse highlights a troublesome corollary to the belief that the Lord punishes sin. The Lord moved the land by His punishment of sin. The same Lord is now invoked to heal it.
II. Do the ones who cause our grief also at times hold the key to resolving it?
III. If this is outside of our control, how can we deal with it constructively?

Grief Relief from the Bible, 56

90. The Lord did not "grieve His words" against Egypt by leaving them unfulfilled.

Psalms 104:28 He sent
shadows and darkened.
He did not grieve His words.

I. This Psalm is a recitation of the mighty works the Lord performed delivering Israel from slavery in Egypt.
II. The Psalmist speaks this about the words the Lord had spoken, warning Egypt to release Israel. After speaking them, the Lord brought them about in fact.
III. Do we still experience the Lord as being true to His promises? How does this impact our grief?

91. The Psalmist's grief causes him to suspect that all men are liars.

Psalms 115:1 Alleluia. I believed
because of what I said,
yet I was greatly humbled.
115:2 I said in my grief,
"Every man *is a* liar."

I. Sometimes in the heat of grief we believe, say, and do things that are extreme, that under normal circumstances we wouldn't.
II. Given that, how can we guard against it when we grieve?
III. How can we make allowances for this when others grieve?

92. In once again gathering Israel and restoring Jerusalem, the Lord will bind up the people's grief.

Psalms 146:2 Building Jerusalem,
the Lord will gather Israel's scattered,
146:3 who heals *the* contrite in heart,
and binds up their griefs...

I. Despite the nation's grief after the Babylonian conquest and captivity, the Lord promised to rebuild and re-gather the people. This actually happened.
II. How do we hold on to God's promises while grieving?

93. Jesus reminds those who question Him that wedding guests don't grieve during the wedding. When the wedding is over, then they will grieve.

Matthew 9:15 Jesus said to them, "Can *the* groom's sons grieve while *the* groom is with them? Days will come when *the* groom will be taken away from them, and they will fast then.

I. Jesus' presence itself is joy in the lives of His disciples.
II. When that sense of His presence fades, then they grieve.
III. How can we as contemporary disciples cultivate a sense of His ongoing presence?

94. A rich young ruler grieves over his possessions after Jesus invites him to sell them and follow Him.

> **Mark 10:21** Jesus, knowing him, loved him, and said to him, "One *thing* is lacking to you. Go, sell whatever you have, and give to *the* poor – and you'll have treasure in *the* sky. Then come follow me!" **10:22** Saddened at *the* word, he went out grieving, for he was holding on to many possessions. **10:23** Looking around, Jesus said to his disciples, "How hard *it is* for *those* who hold on to money to go into God's kingdom!"

I. **This passage highlights** how grievous the prospect of losing our material wealth and possessions can be.
II. **What possessions of ours** would grieve us most to lose?
III. **How ought knowing this** change our attitude toward those things?

95. Mary Magdalene tells the grieving disciples that she has seen the risen Lord, yet they do not believe her.

> **Mark 16:9** Rising up early *the* first *day* after *the* Sabbath, he appeared first to Mary Madgalene, from whom he'd thrown out seven demons. **16:10** Going *back*, she told those who were with him, *while they were* grieving and weeping. **16:11** Hearing that he was alive and had been seen by her, they didn't believe.

I. **Here, Mary Magdalene** is the first to see the risen Christ, yet His disciples are so blinded by their grief that they refuse to believe her.
II. **Sometimes our grief** can blind us even to the best of good news.
III. **Has this ever happened** to us, or to someone we know? How do we guard against that?

Grief Relief from the Bible, 59

Grief in Luke

96. Jesus tells His hearers that this generation is unable to grieve even in pretense.

> **Luke 7:31** "To whom, then, will I compare this generation's men, and to whom are they like? **7:32** They are like boys sitting in *the* market, talking to each other, and saying, 'We played pipes for you, and you didn't dance. We grieved, and you didn't cry.' **7:33** John *the* Baptist came neither eating bread nor drinking wine, and you say, 'He has *a* demon.' **7:34** Man's Son came eating and drinking, and you say, 'Look! *The* man *is a* glutton and wine drinker, *a* friend of tax collectors and sinners.' **7:35** Yet wisdom is justified by all her sons."

I. Some are so preoccupied with worldly affairs that they lose the capacity to grieve.
II. Is the ability to grieve a blessing or a curse in our lives? If we don't have it, what do we lose?

97. Those who love Jesus grieve as He is led out to crucifixion.

> **Luke 23:26** When they were leading him *away*, they seized *a* certain Cyrenian, Simon, coming from *the* countryside, and they set *the* cross on him to carry after Jesus. **23:27** *A* large crowd of people was following him, and women who were crying and grieving him.

I. When we witness a tragedy unfolding before our eyes, grieving is a natural response.
II. When has watching an unfolding tragedy grieved us, even if we weren't able to make a difference in it?
III. How do we cope with such griefs when they are beyond our ability to influence?

Grief Relief from the Bible, 60

98. Ephesian Christians grieve greatly when Paul tells them they will not see his face again.

> **Acts 20:37** Great weeping came from all, and throwing themselves on Paul's neck, they kissed him, **20:38** grieving greatly at *the* word that he said, that they would not see his face further. They led him to *the* ship.

I. The great evangelist Paul spent three years working among the Ephesians. Here, he is on his way to Jerusalem, having been warned repeatedly by the Holy Spirit of what awaits him there. With that in mind, he tells these dear friends that they would not see each other again.

II. We naturally grieve separation from those that we love and admire. What is our consolation in such circumstances?

III. Are there times when we must push ahead, even though it grieves us and others?

99. Paul insists the gravity of the sin among the Corinthian Christians should leave them not proud, but grieving.

> **1 Corinthians 5:1** It is heard altogether *there* is fornication among you, and such fornication as is not among *the* nations – so that someone has *his* father's wife. **5:2** Are you puffed up? Hadn't you rather grieve, so *the one* who did this work may be taken away from among you?

I. Here, Paul writes to an overconfident Corinthian church, rebuking them for the sin that is in their midst. Notice that despite the rebuke, Paul still loves the Christians of Corinth and doesn't give up on them.

II. Do we sometimes celebrate and feel pride when what we ought to feel is grief? How do we guard against this?

III. Have we ever had someone continue loving us, despite our failures? Have we ever done that for others?

Grief Relief from the Bible, 62

100. The writer reminds his readers that discipline is grievous in the moment, but leads to joy.

Hebrews 12:11 Every discipline is seen in *the* present not to be *a* joy, but *a* grief. Yet afterwards, it returns *the* most peaceful fruit through it by *the* practice of righteousness.

I. The writer of Hebrews reminds us that grief is never a happy feeling, yet godly grief leads to a reward all the same.
II. What is godly grief? If one feels it, what other griefs does it enable us to avoid?

Grief Relief from the Bible, 63

101. James urges his readers to humble themselves before the Lord, grieve their sins, and be forgiven.

> **James 4:8** Come near *the* Lord, and He will come near you! Clean *the* hands, sinners, and purify hearts, *you* double-souled! **4:9** Be merciful, and mourn, and weep! Let your laughter be changed into mourning, and joy into grieving! **4:10** Be humbled in *the* Lord's sight, and He will lift you up!

I. The early Christians were often criticized by their pagan neighbors for refusing to participate in the lifestyles of the culture around them. They were mocked for their abhorrence of sin.
II. Yet James saw grief for sin as an essential part of their Christian living.
III. Do we grieve for sin? If we do not, ought we?

102. All earth's tribes will grieve over their rejection of the Lord when they see Him coming in power and glory.

> **Revelation 1:7** Look! He comes with clouds, and every eye will see Him, and *those* who pierced Him. All earth's tribes also will grieve themselves over Him. Even *so*, Amen!

I. According to John, those who so confidently reject Christ in this world will grieve over that fact when they see Him face-to-face.
II. This grief is avoidable, if we will turn to Him. Will we?
III. What is our responsibility toward those who as yet have not turned to Him?

103. Earth's kings, traders, and helmsmen will grieve over Rome's destruction, when their opportunities for power and enrichment come to a crashing end.

> **Revelation 18:7** "As much as she glorified herself and was in luxuries, so give her torment and mourning, because she says in her heart, 'I sit *a* queen, and I am not *a* widow, and I will not see mourning.' **18:8** Therefore, her plagues will come in one day: death and grieving and hunger. She will be burned with fire, because God who has judged her is mighty. **18:9** "Earth's kings who fornicated and lived in luxuries with her will weep and grieve over her when they see *the* smoke of her burning, **18:10** standing far off for fear of her torments, saying,
> 'Woe, woe, that great city Babylon,
> that mighty city –
> for your judgment has come in one hour!'
> **18:11** "Earth's traders will weep and mourn over her, because no one buys their goods any longer: **18:12** goods of gold and silver and precious stones and pearls and fine flax and purple and silk and scarlet, all citrus wood and all ivory vessels and all vessels of precious stone and bronze and iron and marble; **18:13** cinnamon and spice and perfumes and ointments and incense and wine and oil and fine flour and wheat and cattle and sheep and horses and four-wheeled wagons and captives and mens' souls.
> **18:14** "*The* fruit of your soul's desire has pulled away from you. All fatness and light have perished from you, and already you will find them no further. **18:15** Sellers of these who have become rich from them will stand far off crying and grieving, for fear of her torments
> **18:16** and saying,
> 'Woe, woe, that great city,
> who was wrapped in fine linen
> and purple and scarlet,
> and was gilded with gold
> and precious stone and pearls!

18:17 In one hour so many riches
were stripped away!'
"Every helmsman and all who sail into *the* place, sailors and those who work *the* sea stood
far off. **18:18** They cried out, seeing *the* place of her burning, saying, "Who *is* like this great
city?' **18:19** They threw dust on their heads, and cried out, weeping and grieving, saying,
'Woe, woe, great city, in whom all who have
ships on *the* sea have become rich!
She is made desolate in one hour
from her precious things!
18:20 Exult over her,
sky, and holy ones, apostles and prophets,
for God has judged your judgment
against her!'"

I. Here, the ungodly who grew rich dealing with the Roman world grieve when their opportunity to grow even richer
is taken away.
II. What ought they have grieved instead?
III. Are we grieving for the right things in life?

104. God will bring His people's grief to an end when He makes all things new.

> **Revelation 21:4** God will wipe away every tear from their eyes. Death will be no longer,
> nor grieving, nor outcry, nor will pain be *there* any more – because *the* first *things* have gone
> away."

I. This verse in the second-to-last chapter of the Bible sets out the great hope each Christian has in the face of grief.
II. God Himself, who was the first to grieve over sin, will bring this world we know to an end and comfort His people
forever.
III. How do we take this to heart now?

Grief Relief from the Bible, 66

Table of Grief Passages in Scripture

Book	# of Texts	Section	First #	Last #	Order from LTPB
Genesis	11	Torah	1	11	1
Leviticus	2	Torah	12	13	2
Numbers	1	Torah	14	14	3
Deuteronomy	3	Torah	15	17	4
1 Samuel	1	Nevi'im	18	18	5
2 Samuel	5	Nevi'im	19	23	6
Isaiah	11	Nevi'im	24	34	7
Jeremiah	13	Nevi'im	35	47	8
Ezekiel	11	Nevi'im	48	58	9
Hosea	2	Nevi'im	59	60	10
Joel	1	Nevi'im	61	61	11
Amos	2	Nevi'im	62	63	12
Jonah	1	Nevi'im	64	64	13
Micah	2	Nevi'im	65	66	14
Nahum	1	Nevi'im	67	67	15
Habakkuk	1	Nevi'im	68	68	16
Zechariah	2	Nevi'im	69	70	17
Lamentations	2	Kethuvim	71	72	18
Ezra	1	Kethuvim	73	73	19
Nehemiah	1	Kethuvim	74	74	20
Esther	2	Kethuvim	75	76	21
Job	4	Kethuvim	77	80	22
Proverbs	5	Kethuvim	81	85	23
Ecclesiastes	1	Kethuvim	86	86	24
Psalms	6	Kethuvim	87	92	25
Matthew	1	Gospel	93	93	26
Mark	2	Gospel	94	95	27
Luke	2	Gospel	96	97	28
Acts	1	History	98	98	29
1 Corinthians	1	Epistle	99	99	30
Hebrews	1	Epistle	100	100	31
James	1	Epistle	101	101	32
Revelation	3	Apocalypse	102	104	33

Also from Searchlight Press

GOSPELS: MATTHEW, MARK, LUKE, JOHN
A Greek-English, Verse by Verse Translation
(Searchlight Press, 2017)

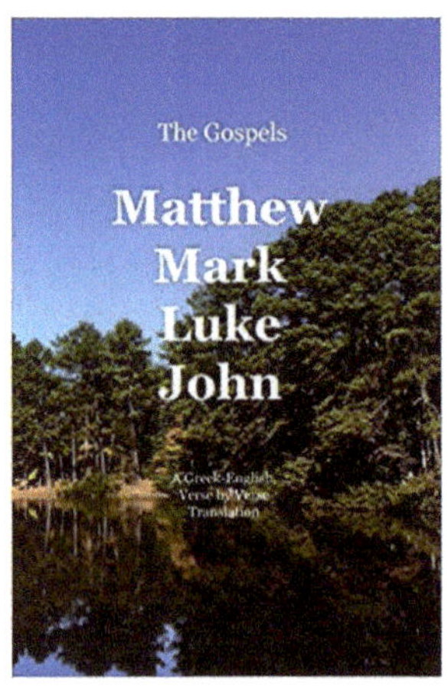

THE LATIN TESTAMENT PROJECT BIBLE
An English Translation of the Vulgate
(Searchlight Press, 2016)

THE LATIN TESTAMENT PROJECT NEW TESTAMENT
A Latin-English, Verse by Verse Translation
(Searchlight Press, 2013)

WONDERWORKING POWER:
A Fresh Translation of the Gospel of Mark
(Searchlight Press, 2011)